# How Fiona

## became a

# Unicorn

For Jasmine, my favorite

unicorn ever  ♡ ♡ ♡

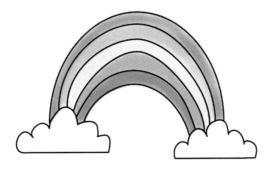

Liliya Glavatskyy

Once upon a time, there was a family of horses: daddy horse, mommy horse, and five baby horses. The names of the siblings were **C**innamon, **S**pirit, **R**io, **D**ollie, and **F**iona.

They lived in a forest and loved spending their days enjoying the sunshine and running up and down the hills playing horse games.

2

3

The big day was coming up for the baby horses: They were about to turn **ONE** year old. There was so much excitement about their upcoming birthday party!

Mommy horse was preparing to bake a big birthday cake, and daddy horse was making gifts for the baby horses.

One evening, when the baby horses were laying in their beds and talking happily about their upcoming birthday party, suddenly Rio said,

"Guys, look at Fiona! What's that bump on her forehead?"

Cinnamon, Rio, Spirit, and Dollie all jumped up from their beds and gathered around Fiona.

"Oh! Fiona, is that bump hurting you?" asked Rio.

"It's so big, sister!" cried Spirit.

"Can you push it back inside?" asked Cinnamon and pressed on Fiona's forehead.

"I'm wondering if it's gonna go away before the birthday party..." said quietly Dollie.

6

Poor Fiona was almost in tears! She hadn't noticed the bump before, but now it was definitely there, hard and pointy. Oh, how would she look for her big party?! Fiona wanted to cry...

When Fiona's brothers and sister were asleep, Fiona sat up in her bed and touched her own forehead again. The bump had gotten bigger!!! Oh no! Their birthday party was in three days!

In the morning, when everyone was gathering to eat breakfast, Fiona showed up with a hat on her head. It was very cute and had flowers on it.

"I love your hat, Fiona!" exclaimed Dollie.

"Can I try it on?" Dollie grabbed the hat before Fiona had a chance to say no.

11

"What happened to the bump?! It's **HUGE!**" cried Spirit.

Fiona got so overwhelmed. She felt sad and scared. So she just ran away.

Fiona ran for many hours without stopping. She was crying and couldn't see clearly where she was going.

When it got dark outside, Fiona didn't know which way her home was. Exhausted, she laid down and fell asleep.

At home, Fiona's parents were heartbroken and worried about their baby girl. They searched the forest all around but couldn't find her.

"Fiona!!!" yelled her brothers and sister.

"Where are you?! Come home!"

But Fiona was nowhere to be found...

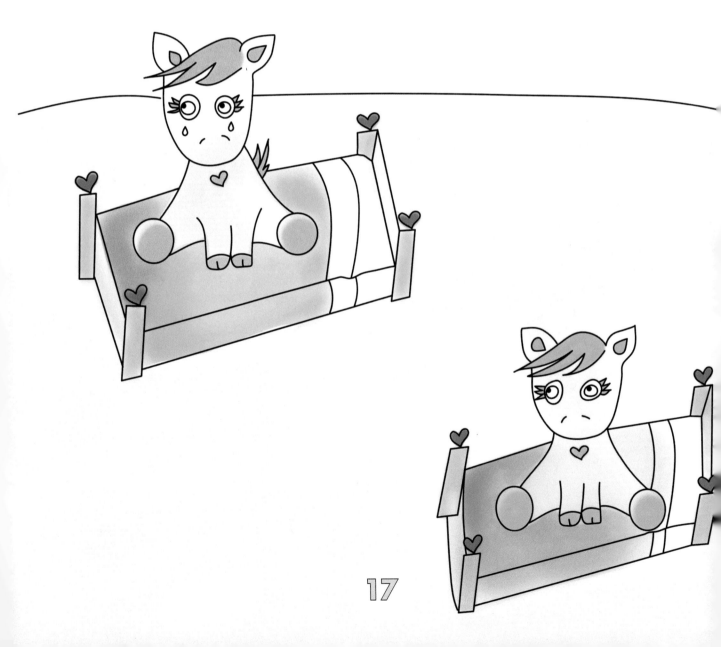

On the morning of the third day, everyone woke up in a bad mood. It was the baby horses' birthday, but nobody could think about the party. The parents were too worried that their baby girl Fiona was still missing.

Meanwhile, Fiona kept walking, looking for her home and family. She was so tired and scared. She wanted to be with her mommy, daddy, and her brothers and sister.

"Fiona!!!!" Cinnamon was the first one to notice his sister.
"Baby girl, you are back!!!" cried mommy and daddy.
"We were so scared and kept looking for you everywhere."

21

"What's that on your head, Fiona?" asked Dollie. Fiona touched her forehead carefully. The bump was bigger, much BIGGER and it was hard to the touch.

"It's so BEAUTIFUL!!!" cried Cinnamon, Spirit, Rio, and Dollie all at once.

"You are a UNICORN, baby girl. You're so special and you're so beautiful" said mommy and daddy.

Fiona's horn glowed pretty golden colors.

Fiona was happy to be back home. She had missed her family so much!

And she was just in time for her FIRST birthday party. It was a fun day for the whole family. The siblings were so excited and so proud to have a real unicorn as their sister.

# THE END

62320074R00018

Made in the USA
Columbia, SC
01 July 2019